Francis Frith's
AROUND BRISTOL

◆

PHOTOGRAPHIC MEMORIES

Francis Frith's
AROUND BRISTOL

◆

Clive Hardy

First published in the United Kingdom in 1999 by
Frith Book Company Ltd

Hardback Edition 1999
ISBN 1-85937-050-0

Paperback Edition 2001
ISBN 1-85937-264-3

Hardback Reprinted 2001
ISBN 1-85937-050-0

British Library Cataloguing in Publication Data

Francis Frith's Around Bristol
Clive Hardy

Frith Book Company Ltd
Frith's Barn, Teffont,
Salisbury, Wiltshire SP3 5QP
Tel: +44 (0) 1722 716 376
Email: info@frithbook.co.uk
www.frithbook.co.uk

Printed and bound in Great Britain

AS WITH ANY HISTORICAL DATABASE THE FRITH ARCHIVE IS CONSTANTLY BEING CORRECTED AND IMPROVED
AND THE PUBLISHERS WOULD WELCOME INFORMATION ON OMISSIONS OR INACCURACIES

CONTENTS

Francis Frith: Victorian Pioneer   7

Frith's Archive - A Unique Legacy   10

Bristol - An Introduction   12

Around the City   18

Bristol Docks and Avonmouth   59

Clifton   71

Around and About   81

Index   88

Free Mounted Print Voucher

FRANCIS FRITH: *Victorian Pioneer*

FRANCIS FRITH, Victorian founder of the world-famous photographic archive, was a complex and multitudinous man. A devout Quaker and a highly successful Victorian businessman, he was both philosophic by nature and pioneering in outlook.

By 1855 Francis Frith had already established a wholesale grocery business in Liverpool, and sold it for the astonishing sum of £200,000, which is the equivalent today of over £15,000,000. Now a multi-millionaire, he was able to indulge his passion for travel. As a child he had pored over travel books written by early explorers, and his fancy and imagination had been stirred by family holidays to the sublime mountain regions of Wales and Scotland. 'What a land of spirit-stirring and enriching scenes and places!' he had written. He was to return to these scenes of grandeur in later years to 'recapture the thousands of vivid and tender memories', but with a different purpose. Now in his thirties, and captivated by the new science of photography, Frith set out on a series of pioneering journeys to the Nile regions that occupied him from 1856 until 1860.

INTRIGUE AND ADVENTURE

He took with him on his travels a specially-designed wicker carriage that acted as both dark-room and sleeping chamber. These far-flung journeys were packed with intrigue and adventure. In his life story, written when he was sixty-three, Frith tells of being held captive by bandits, and of fighting 'an awful midnight battle to the very point of surrender with a deadly pack of hungry, wild dogs'. Sporting flowing Arab costume, Frith arrived at Akaba by camel seventy years before Lawrence, where he encountered 'desert princes and rival sheikhs, blazing with jewel-hilted swords'.

During these extraordinary adventures he was assiduously exploring the desert regions bordering the Nile and patiently recording the antiquities and peoples with his camera. He was the first photographer to venture beyond the sixth cataract. Africa was still the mysterious 'Dark Continent', and Stanley and Livingstone's historic meeting was a decade into the future. The conditions for picture taking confound belief. He laboured for hours in his wicker dark-room in the sweltering heat of the desert, while the volatile chemicals fizzed dangerously in their trays. Often he was forced to work in remote tombs and caves

where conditions were cooler. Back in London he exhibited his photographs and was 'rapturously cheered' by members of the Royal Society. His reputation as a photographer was made overnight. An eminent modern historian has likened their impact on the population of the time to that on our own generation of the first photographs taken on the surface of the moon.

VENTURE OF A LIFE-TIME

Characteristically, Frith quickly spotted the opportunity to create a new business as a specialist publisher of photographs. He lived in an era of immense and sometimes violent change. For the poor in the early part of Victoria's reign work was a drudge and the hours long, and people had precious little free time to enjoy themselves.

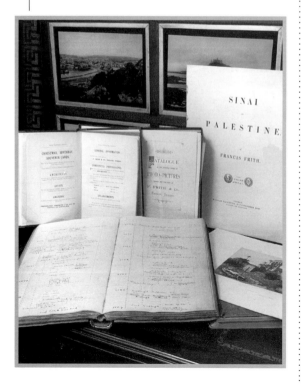

Most had no transport other than a cart or gig at their disposal, and had not travelled far beyond the boundaries of their own town or village. However, by the 1870s, the railways had threaded their way across the country, and Bank Holidays and half-day Saturdays had been made obligatory by Act of Parliament. All of a sudden the ordinary working man and his family were able to enjoy days out and see a little more of the world.

With characteristic business acumen, Francis Frith foresaw that these new tourists would enjoy having souvenirs to commemorate their days out. In 1860 he married Mary Ann Rosling and set out with the intention of photographing every city, town and village in Britain. For the next thirty years he travelled the country by train and by pony and trap, producing fine photographs of seaside resorts and beauty spots that were keenly bought by millions of Victorians. These prints were painstakingly pasted into family albums and pored over during the dark nights of winter, rekindling precious memories of summer excursions.

THE RISE OF FRITH & CO

Frith's studio was soon supplying retail shops all over the country. To meet the demand he gathered about him a small team of photographers, and published the work of independent artist-photographers of the calibre of Roger Fenton and Francis Bedford. In order to gain some understanding of the scale of Frith's business one only has to look at the catalogue issued by Frith & Co in 1886: it runs to some 670

pages, listing not only many thousands of views of the British Isles but also many photographs of most European countries, and China, Japan, the USA and Canada – note the sample page shown above from the hand-written *Frith & Co* ledgers detailing pictures taken. By 1890 Frith had created the greatest specialist photographic publishing company in the world, with over 2,000 outlets – more than the combined number that Boots and WH Smith have today! The picture on the right shows the *Frith & Co* display board at Ingleton in the Yorkshire Dales. Beautifully constructed with mahogany frame and gilt inserts, it could display up to a dozen local scenes.

POSTCARD BONANZA

The ever-popular holiday postcard we know today took many years to develop. In 1870 the Post Office issued the first plain cards, with a pre-printed stamp on one face. In 1894 they allowed other publishers' cards to be sent through the mail with an attached adhesive halfpenny stamp. Demand grew rapidly, and in 1895 a new size of postcard was permitted called the

court card, but there was little room for illustration. In 1899, a year after Frith's death, a new card measuring 5.5 x 3.5 inches became the standard format, but it was not until 1902 that the divided back came into being, with address and message on one face and a full-size illustration on the other. *Frith & Co* were in the vanguard of postcard development, and Frith's sons Eustace and Cyril continued their father's monumental task, expanding the number of views offered to the public and recording more and more places in Britain, as the coasts and countryside were opened up to mass travel.

Francis Frith died in 1898 at his villa in Cannes, his great project still growing. The archive he created continued in business for another seventy years. By 1970 it contained over a third of a million pictures of 7,000 cities, towns and villages. The massive photographic record Frith has left to us stands as a living monument to a special and very remarkable man.

Frith's Archive: *A Unique Legacy*

FRANCIS FRITH'S legacy to us today is of immense significance and value, for the magnificent archive of evocative photographs he created provides a unique record of change in 7,000 cities, towns and villages throughout Britain over a century and more. Frith and his fellow studio photographers revisited locations many times down the years to update their views, compiling for us an enthralling and colourful pageant of British life and character.

We tend to think of Frith's sepia views of Britain as nostalgic, for most of us use them to conjure up memories of places in our own lives with which we have family associations. It often makes us forget that to Francis Frith they were records of daily life as it was actually being lived in the cities, towns and villages of his day. The Victorian age was one of great and often bewildering change for ordinary people, and though the pictures evoke an impression of slower times, life was as busy and hectic as it is today.

We are fortunate that Frith was a photographer of the people, dedicated to recording the minutiae of everyday life. For it is this sheer wealth of visual data, the painstaking chronicle of changes in dress, transport, street layouts, buildings, housing, engineering and landscape that captivates us so much today. His remarkable images offer us a powerful link with the past and with the lives of our ancestors.

TODAY'S TECHNOLOGY

Computers have now made it possible for Frith's many thousands of images to be accessed almost instantly. In the Frith archive today, each photograph is carefully 'digitised' then stored on a CD Rom. Frith archivists can locate a single photograph amongst thousands within seconds. Views can be catalogued and sorted under a variety of categories of place and content to the immediate benefit of researchers. Inexpensive reference prints can be created for them at the touch of a mouse button, and a wide range of books and other printed materials assembled and published for a wider, more general readership - in the next twelve months over a hundred Frith local history titles will be published! The

See Frith at www. francisfrith.co.uk

day-to-day workings of the archive are very different from how they were in Francis Frith's time: imagine the herculean task of sorting through eleven tons of glass negatives as Frith had to do to locate a particular sequence of pictures! Yet the archive still prides itself on maintaining the same high standards of excellence laid down by Francis Frith, including the painstaking cataloguing and indexing of every view.

It is curious to reflect on how the internet now allows researchers in America and elsewhere greater instant access to the archive than Frith himself ever enjoyed. Many thousands of individual views can be called up on screen within seconds on one of the Frith internet sites, enabling people living continents away to revisit the streets of their ancestral home town, or view places in Britain where they have enjoyed holidays. Many overseas researchers welcome the chance to view special theme selections, such as transport, sports, costume and ancient monuments.

We are certain that Francis Frith would have heartily approved of these modern developments, for he himself was always working at the very limits of Victorian photographic technology.

THE VALUE OF THE ARCHIVE TODAY

Because of the benefits brought by the computer, Frith's images are increasingly studied by social historians, by researchers into genealogy and ancestory, by architects, town planners, and by teachers and schoolchildren involved in local history projects. In addition, the archive offers every one of us a unique opportunity to examine the places where we and our families have lived and worked down the years. Immensely successful in Frith's own era, the archive is now, a century and more on, entering a new phase of popularity.

THE PAST IN TUNE WITH THE FUTURE

Historians consider the Francis Frith Collection to be of prime national importance. It is the only archive of its kind remaining in private ownership and has been valued at a million pounds. However, this figure is now rapidly increasing as digital technology enables more and more people around the world to enjoy its benefits.

Francis Frith's archive is now housed in an historic timber barn in the beautiful village of Teffont in Wiltshire. Its founder would not recognize the archive office as it is today. In place of the many thousands of dusty boxes containing glass plate negatives and an all-pervading odour of photographic chemicals, there are now ranks of computer screens. He would be amazed to watch his images travelling round the world at unimaginable speeds through network and internet lines.

The archive's future is both bright and exciting. Francis Frith, with his unshakeable belief in making photographs available to the greatest number of people, would undoubtedly approve of what is being done today with his lifetime's work. His photographs, depicting our shared past, are now bringing pleasure and enlightenment to millions around the world a century and more after his death.

BRISTOL – *An Introduction*

THIS FAMOUS old city, situated seven miles up the Avon from the Bristol Channel, rose to become the second most important city in England after London. As early as the 10th century there was a mint, and in 1373 it was designated as a county in its own right. But it was the navigable Rivers Avon and Severn that gave Bristol its competitive edge; by the 12th century there was an established wine trade with the Bordeaux region, which was soon extended to Spain. In 1445 the Mariners' Guild was founded, and the Fellowship of Merchants was set up in 1500. In 1552 the Merchant Venturers were incorporated, and from then on sea-going Bristol ships could, theoretically, be found anywhere in the known world. Though most were involved in the trade with Spain, during the grain shortages of the 1580s several ships made trips to the Baltic.

During the Civil War, the possession of Bristol was vital to the King's cause. While the Royal Standard flew over the second most important city in England, the diplomatic initiatives to obtain foreign military assistance had currency. If it fell, then the King's cause would be seriously undermined. On 15 March 1643 Sir William Waller, with a force of fewer than 2,000 Parliamentary troops, had managed to secure the city, but the following July he was badly defeated at Roundway Down and his army was all but destroyed. Prince Rupert marched on Bristol, whose garrison had been stripped by Waller prior to his defeat, and summoned its defenders, under Colonel Nathaniel Fiennes, to surrender. Fiennes rejected the offer and two days later the Royalists attacked. Despite an outstanding defence, which inflicted heavy casualties on the Royalists, Fiennes had little hope of holding out and had no alternative but to ask for terms. Magnanimous in victory, Rupert allowed the garrison to march out of the city with the full honours of war: drums beating and flags flying. Despite his stand, Fiennes was tried the following August and condemned to death, though he was later reprieved.

Bristol now became the major Royalist base in the West Country for both land and naval operations, and a port for blockade runners bringing weapons and supplies from Europe. Mindful of Fiennes' difficulties in defending a city with a large perimeter, Prince Rupert set about strengthening the defences, which included the construction of the Royal Fort on Windmill Hill.

Following the battle of Marston Moor, Rupert returned to Bristol in October 1644 to organize defences and prepare for an expected siege; this came the following August, after the Royalist disaster at Naseby. Ordering the burning of Clifton, Bedminster and Westbury, Rupert pulled his forces into the city. Though Rupert wrote to the King promising to hold Bristol, his own combat experience must have told him that it was a hopeless cause. After putting up stiff resistance, the parleying for

Austrian Succession and the Seven Years War, the wet dock at Sea Mills was used as a privateer base. During the American War of Independence, 157 Bristol ships sailed under letters of marque, and during the French Revolution and the Napoleonic Wars, the city furnished a total of 63 privateers.

Not all the slaves handled by Bristol were from Africa. From the early years of the 17th century, thousands of men and women were sentenced by English courts to servitude in the colonies of the New World; the majority were destined to work on plantations. It was

terms began on 4 September 1645, with the final surrender occurring on the 10th. With the loss of Bristol it could be argued that the war was lost.

PRIVATEERS AND SLAVERS

During the 18th century a large number of Bristol vessels undertook voyages as privateers. Sailing under letters of marque, a privateer was a privately armed vessel, authorized to wage war upon the king's enemies, in return for prize money. During the War of the

soon realized, however, that if the plantation system was to be maintained and expanded an alternative source of labour had to be found, and by 1619 the first cargoes of negro slaves were landed. Until the Restoration, slaving was carried on by English, Dutch and a few colonial ships, but the majority of merchants involved in the Guinea trade, as it was called, were more interested in gold and ivory than in human cargo.

Things changed in the 1660s with the establishment of the joint-stock Royal African Company. From now on, slaving would become the main traffic. The Royal African Company tried to maintain a monopoly on the slave trade, and though a few Bristol merchants held shares in it, most were for free trade, and were of the opinion that any competent captain could cruise the West African coast, slaving at will. And this is precisely what most of them did. Despite a petition from the Royal African Company, Parliament threw the slave trade open to anyone prepared to pay 10 per cent tax on a voyage. In 1707-08, of the 52 ships that cleared Bristol to take part in the Guinea trade, fifty were free traders. In 1725 Bristol cleared 63 ships with a total capacity for 16,950 slaves, and though twenty years later the number of ships had been reduced to 47, the carrying capacity had dropped by only 310 slaves.

Though Bristol and London controlled slaving, they were soon to be eclipsed by a new player, Liverpool. With a different pay structure in operation, Liverpool ships were more profitable per voyage than their rivals at London and Bristol. In 1753 Liverpool cleared 63 slavers, Bristol 27, London 13, Lancaster 7, Glasgow 4, Chester 1, and Plymouth 1. Between 1756 and 1786, a total of 588 slaving voyages were made from Bristol, while Liverpool vessels made 1,858.

The slavers did not always have it their own way. In 1759, a slave ship operating along the Gambia River was attacked and boarded by natives. The captain who was badly wounded, and seeing that his ship was about to be overrun, made his way to the powder magazine and fired his pistol into it. The ship blew up killing everyone on board.

In May 1750, the Bristol slaver 'King David' was overrun by slaves who had managed to break into the arms locker. The captain and five crewmen were killed, while the rest took refuge in the hold. The leader of the slaves, who spoke good English, told the surviving crewmen that if they came up on deck they would be spared, but as each man came topside he was put in irons and given Jonah's toss (thrown overboard). The mate was the last to come up, and was only spared when it was realized that there was no one else left who knew how to handle the ship or navigate.

Bristol continued to send ships to West Africa that were unconnected with the slave trade, but there were never many of them. In 1840, some of the ships clearing Bristol included 45 for the West Indies, 14 for Newfoundland, 14 for West Africa, 9 for Canada, 7 for Australia and 3 for the East Indies. In 1835, a cargo of tea was landed directly from Canton, but attempts to establish the Bristol Tea Co and offer an alternative port to London failed.

By the early decades of the 19th century, Bristol was suffering and losing out to London, Liverpool and Hull, owing to the high charges imposed by the dock company. In 1840, Bristol had at least seven ships operating on the route to Australia, but docking dues, which were seven times greater than that charged by Liverpool, killed the traffic. Exports to Australia remained, but on a small scale.

It was only in the 20th century that Bristol, thanks to the development of Avonmouth, managed to return to something like the bustling days of the 18th century. In 1890, it was selected as the UK port for the fortnightly Imperial West Indies mail service, and from 1921 liners from Rangoon and Colombo were making scheduled calls at Avonmouth. An important boost for Avonmouth came in 1901 when Elders & Fyffes inaugurated their fortnightly service to Port Limon, Costa Rica. For over sixty years the banana ships would use Avonmouth, which involved the railways in operating over 400 special banana trains a year. Following the completion of the Royal Edward Dock in 1908, Avonmouth continued to expand.

In 1911, twenty-seven oil storage tanks were installed near the docks, and an oil basin was added in 1919. Between 1922-23 the eastern arm of the Royal Edward was built, alongside which were constructed large transit sheds and granaries. In 1938 the docks handled 51 ships carrying 231,000 tons of fruit, oilseeds, rice and tea from India, Burma, Ceylon and Malaya, while a further 86 ships discharged over 200,000 tons of cargo from Australia and New Zealand. The total for the year was 354 ships with more than one million tons of cargo landed.

Matthew's Bristol Directory of 1828 states that 'Bristol is ranked the second city in England in respect of riches, trade and population'. Things were about to change.

Industrialization would see obscure places like Middlesbrough, which had a population of less than fifty people, expand in less than one hundred years to a town of over 90,000 inhabitants. In 1700, Bristol's population was approximately 20,000 which would put it in third place behind London and Norwich. By 1800, with a population of 60,000, it had slipped to sixth place, and by 1850, with 137,000 inhabitants, it would be ranked seventh. In terms of being a port, Bristol was, in 1700, the second largest in England. By 1800 it had dropped to eighth, but by 1855 had pulled back to sixth largest, but ranked twelfth in terms of overseas trade.

BY ROAD AND RAIL

By the beginning of the 19th century the Bristol Mail from London offered a fast service. The 105 miles from Hyde Park Corner to York House, on the outskirts of Bath, could be covered in just eleven hours. The coach was scheduled to arrive at York House at half-past seven in the morning; after a change of hors-

es, it proceeded through Bath and on to the Bristol road. At the time, this section of road was considered to be the best in all of England, thanks to John Macadam. He had moved to Bristol around 1803, and later became surveyor to the Bristol Turnpike Trust. On crossing the Bristol Bridge, the coach continued up the High Street and then turned into Corn Street, where the post office was situated; the scheduled arrival time was four minutes past nine. Bristol had one of the busiest provincial post offices in the country. There were daily mails to London, Oxford, Birmingham and Portsmouth, as well as a Welsh mail and a West of England mail. The office was also responsible for the initial sorting of overseas mails to and from the Americas, Portugal and most Mediterranean ports. From the various inns in the city, such as the White Hart and the Bush, it has been estimated that over two hundred coaches arrived and departed daily.

Bristol also had a considerable number of haulage firms operating scheduled services as far as Yorkshire and Nottinghamshire. The railways came to Bristol in 1835, with the opening of the southern section of the Bristol & Gloucester Railway, which involved the construction of the 515 yards long Staple Hill Tunnel. The Bristol terminus was at Avonside Wharf on the Floating Harbour. The second railway to enter the city was the Great Western, whose first train ran on the Bristol to Bath section on 31 August 1840. Ten trains operated on the first day, carrying nearly 6,000 passengers and generating revenue to the tune of £476. The line to London was completed in June 1840. The third railway was the Bristol & Exeter, with twelve Bristolians on the sixteen-strong board of directors, and

Isambard Kingdom Brunel appointed as engineer. The line was worked with GWR locomotives and rolling stock, and when it opened throughout, in May 1844, it was the longest main-line in the country: the distance between London and Exeter was 194 miles.

CLIFTON SPA

As well as being a large, prosperous city and port, Bristol, or more accurately Clifton, developed as a spa; the Hotwells proved popular with high society, especially after the discovery of a second spring in 1702. During the 18th century, Clifton became a fashionable resort, and in this part of the country was second only to Bath. The resort had all the amenities one would expect: a pump room and assembly rooms were built in 1722, and even branches of some London shops would open there for the season.

When Thomas Newton was Bishop of Bristol, from 1761 to 1781, the Hotwells were popular with fashionable society, of which some members were Roman Catholic. England at that time was Protestant in all things, and those of the Catholic faith were legally proscribed against in many situations. On hearing that there was a plan to open a 'mass house' at the Hotwells, Bishop Newton called in Bristol's lone Catholic priest, Father Scudamore, for a friendly chat. Having taken government advice on the matter, Bishop Newton left the priest in no doubt whatsoever that if he went ahead, he would feel the full weight of the law.

In 1870 the Docks Committee ordered the demolition of most of the facilities, but even up to the outbreak of the Great War it was estimated that around 350 people a day went to take the waters. The well was finally closed owing to its being contaminated by river water, which was seeping into it. A couple of bore holes were drilled, the aim being to strike the spring further back where, it was hoped, it would be free from pollution, but the enterprise was unsuccessful.

In 1828 Isambard Kingdom Brunel was staying at Clifton for his health, spending much of his time on sketching expeditions along the Gorge. By coincidence, in October 1829 the Merchant Venturers advertised for plans to bridge the Gorge, since money had been left for the purpose by William Vick in 1752. Despite competition from experienced engineers such as Thomas Telford, one of young Isambard's sketches was selected. Brunel's original estimate had been £52,966, but by the time the final design was ready the price had gone up to £57,000. Vick's legacy would not be enough, and it would be August 1836 before the foundation stone was laid.

Brunel's steamships, 'Great Western' and 'Great Britain', were built at Bristol, though both were too big to be able to use the Floating Harbour. The 'Great Western', which pioneered transatlantic steamer services, was a wooden paddle-steamer of 1,340 tons, and though she was based at Kingroad near the mouth of the Avon, the money-grabbing Bristol Dock Co still demanded full port dues on her. The 'Great Britain', being a much larger vessel and built of iron, was immediately based at Liverpool, where she was joined by the 'Great Western' in 1842. Both ships drew large crowds when they were first towed out of Bristol and through the Gorge at Clifton.

KEYNSHAM

During the Monmouth Rebellion of 1685, the bridge over the Avon at Keynsham became vital to the strategic planning of both sides. If Monmouth could take it, he could attack Bristol, which was defended by the Duke of Beaufort who had a few militia units and some regulars at his disposal. If the king's forces could destroy the bridge, Monmouth would be held up for at least a couple of days while it was repaired, though he would still be in a position to attack Bristol before he could be engaged by the bulk of the royalist forces on their way to intercept him. Monmouth would also have had an opportunity to give the royalists the slip by heading for the North via Gloucester.

ST MARY REDCLIFFE 1887 20153

As large as a cathedral and one of only two parish
churches in England to have stone vaulting,
St Mary's was built on a grand scale, thanks to the
generosity of Bristol merchants. The interior is 240ft
in length, 117ft across the transepts, and the spire is
285ft high.

ST MARY REDCLIFFE, NORTH PORCH 1901 46502
The name Redcliffe derives from the red sandstone outcrop on which the church stands, and of which it is mainly
built.

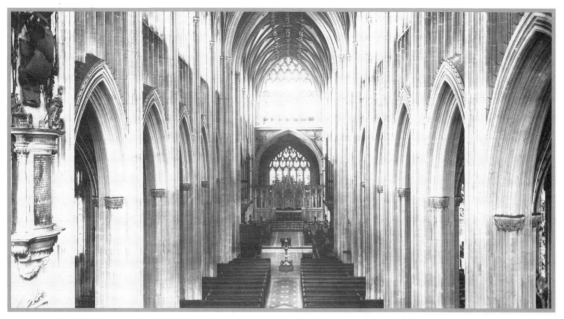

ST MARY REDCLIFFE, THE NAVE 1887 20157

ST MARY REDCLIFFE
The Nave 1887

The stone vaulted nave, looking east.
The church houses some interesting
artefacts, including what is purported to
be a rib from the Dun Cow, said to have
been slain by that old-fashioned
homicidal maniac, Guy of Warwick; it is,
in fact, a whale-bone, thought to have
been presented by Cabot.

◆

ST MARY REDCLIFFE
The Altar 1887

The magnificent St Mary Redcliffe owes
much to the generosity of William
Canynge the elder (died 1396), and his
grandson William Canynge the younger
(1394?-1474). In front of the high altar is
a brass to John Brooke and his wife
Johanna. She was the daughter of
Richard Amerycke, collector for
Customs and patron of John Cabot. So
just who was America named after?

ST MARY REDCLIFFE, THE ALTAR 1887 20159

THE CABOT TOWER 1900 45564
In 1497 John Cabot, under the patronage of Richard Amerycke, sailed from Bristol in the ship 'Matthew'. On 24 June Cabot discovered mainland America, and the following year his son Sebastian explored the American coast from Newfoundland to Florida.

THE CATHEDRAL 1890

The west towers shortly after they had been completed. The Bristol dioceses was created by Henry VIII in 1542, and comprised eighteen parishes within the city boundaries, fourteen others in Gloucestershire, and Abbots Leigh in Somerset. It was refounded by Pope Paul IV in 1557.

THE CATHEDRAL,
The Lady Chapel 1896

Bristol cathedral has two Lady Chapels. The Elder Lady Chapel was built by Abbot David around 1210-1215, and was restored in the 1890s. Originally it was detached from the main building, but was incorporated at some time between 1298 and 1363 when the choir was reconstructed.

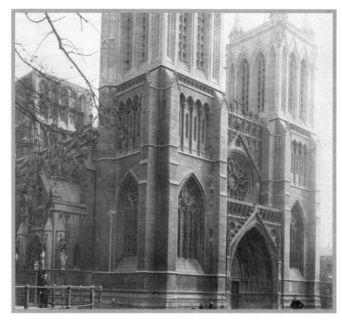

THE CATHEDRAL 1890   24634

THE CATHEDRAL, THE LADY CHAPEL 1896   38171

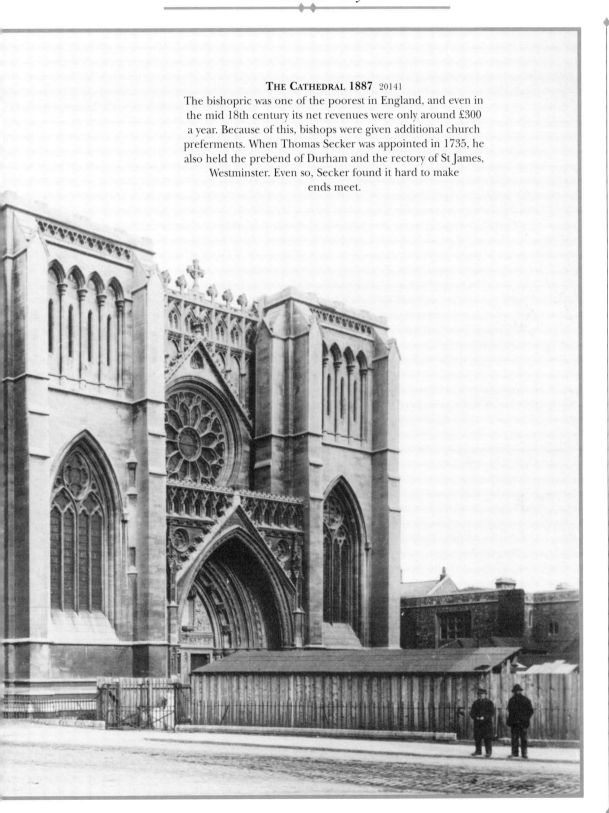

THE CATHEDRAL 1887 20141
The bishopric was one of the poorest in England, and even in
the mid 18th century its net revenues were only around £300
a year. Because of this, bishops were given additional church
preferments. When Thomas Secker was appointed in 1735, he
also held the prebend of Durham and the rectory of St James,
Westminster. Even so, Secker found it hard to make
ends meet.

THE CATHEDRAL, THE NAVE 1900 45572
Because it lacks a clerestory and triforium, the aisles rise to the same height as the nave, a feature making Bristol unique among English cathedrals. The original Norman nave was partially reconstructed at the time of the Dissolution, but then was allowed to fall into ruin. The present nave is 19th century and was built, along with the west towers, between 1868 and 1888.

THE CATHEDRAL, THE CHOIR 1900 45573
This photograph looks east toward the reredos and the stone screen. The reredos was erected in 1899, and is renowned for its skeleton vaulting and stellate tomb recesses.

THE CATHEDRAL, THE CHOIR, WEST 1900 45575
At this date, entry to the main body of the church was free, but the sub-sacrist kept the keys to the Chapter House (considered one of the finest Norman chambers in the country), the Elder Lady Chapel and the Berkeley Chapel. The fee to see these gems was 6d.

COLLEGE GREEN 1887 20128
Originally, College Green was the burial ground for the Augustinian abbey, founded by Robert Fitzhardinge in 1148, and for a hospital, founded jointly by Maurice Berkeley of Gaunt and his nephew, Robert de Gourney. Bristol also had two hospitals for lepers: St Mary Magdelene's, Brightbow, was for women, while a similar institution for men existed to the east of the town boundary.

PARK STREET 1950

The Gothic tower of the university rises above the rooftops. Incorporated in 1909, the main university buildings were paid for by Sir George Arthur Wills and his brother Henry Herbert Wills in memory of their father.

PARK STREET 1900

It was along here that the Philosophical and Literary Institution had its premises in the early years of the 19th century, and one of the first scientific lecturers was Humphrey Davy. Davy also belonged to the Bristol Library Society. Its members included Samuel Taylor Coleridge, Robert Southey and William Wordsworth.

PARK STREET 1950 B212271

PARK STREET 1900 45654

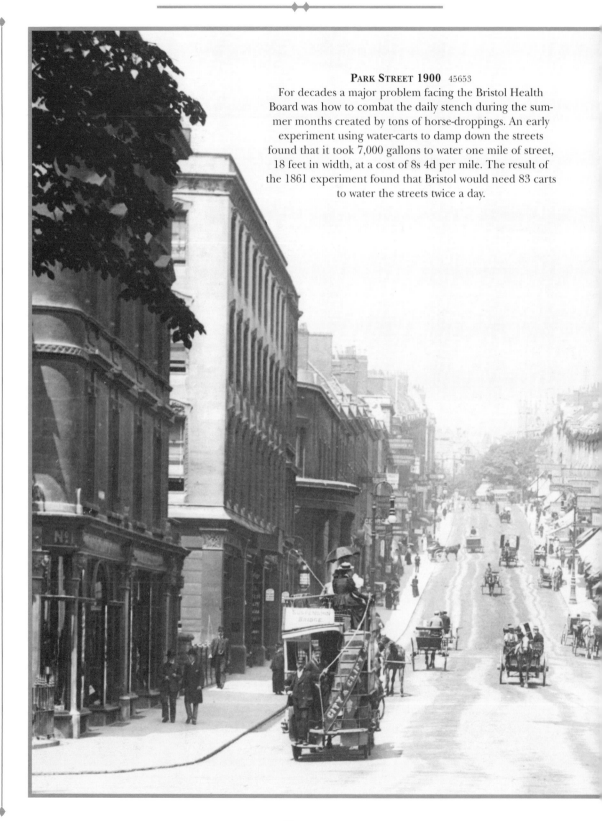

PARK STREET 1900 45653

For decades a major problem facing the Bristol Health Board was how to combat the daily stench during the summer months created by tons of horse-droppings. An early experiment using water-carts to damp down the streets found that it took 7,000 gallons to water one mile of street, 18 feet in width, at a cost of 8s 4d per mile. The result of the 1861 experiment found that Bristol would need 83 carts to water the streets twice a day.

THE UNIVERSITY FROM CABOT TOWER C1950 B212203

THE UNIVERSITY
from Cabot Tower c1950

The university tower was designed by Sir George Oatley, and completed in 1925. Sir George also designed the physics laboratory at the Royal Fort, which was opened by Lord Rutherford in 1927.

QUEENS ROAD 1900

Queens Road, at the top of Park Street, was chosen as the site for both the City Art Gallery and the City Museum. As well as containing works by Gainsborough, Constable and Reynolds, the Art Gallery is also home to Hogarth's altarpiece from St Mary Redcliffe, and Solario's Withypool Triptych, which is dated 1514.

QUEENS ROAD 1900 45653A

ST AUGUSTINE'S BRIDGE 1900 45649
Barrow boys, porters and carters do their best to earn a few shillings. Note the large pair of spectacles above the optician's shop. Victorian retailers were fond of using such devices, which were usually painted gold, to advertise their premises.

BRISTOL, CITY CENTRE c1950 B212258
St Augustine's Parade was an interesting mix of architectural styles and advertisements. Whatever happened to Abdullah cigarettes?

ST AUGUSTINE'S BRIDGE 1901 47886
Bristol's electric tramway system was inaugurated on
14 October 1895. This picture shows several cars at
the terminus near to St Augustine's Bridge. The
tramway was operated by a private company, rather
than the Corporation, until 1937.

ST AUGUSTINE'S BRIDGE 1901 47885

The Tramways Act of 1870 gave powers to Bristol
Corporation to take over the system at book price in 1915, or
at any seventh year thereafter. Every seven years the council
could not get its act together to make a firm commitment.
The result was that the tramway company spent very little on
upgrading the system, and it remained virtually unaltered
throughout its forty-six year existence.

CITY CENTRE 1950 B212227

St Augustine's Bridge looks pretty much the same as it did at the beginning of the 20th century, though the trees have grown, the trams have gone, and there is neither a horse nor a pile of horse muck in sight.

THE CENTRE c1950 B212255

St Augustine's Parade is on the left, and Broad Quay on the right. The area is known locally as 'The Scilly Isles', and was created in 1893 when the decision was taken to fill in a branch of the Floating Harbour.

THE CENTRE c1950 B212283
Judging by the decorations, the picture was taken either shortly before, or just after, the coronation of Queen Elizabeth II.

THE CENTRE c1950 B212265

The half-timbered building on the left is being used by Bristol bus and coach services. The Bristol Tramways and Carriage Co was taken over by the Corporation in 1937. All 237 trams were identical, and all were open-topped. The tramway closed in April 1941 when a bomb destroyed the power supply.

BROAD STREET c1950 B212196

When Celia Fiennes visited Bristol in 1698 she noted that there were nineteen parish churches. There was no official place of worship for Catholics until the 1730s, and even then it was only created out of necessity. Abraham Darby owned a brassworks in the city, but in order to beat off foreign competition he needed to employ skilled Flemish workers; they would only come to Bristol if they were allowed to worship freely as Catholics.

OLD HOUSES AND TOLLEY'S BANK 1890 24641
The junction of Wine Street and High Street. High Street was where Joseph Cottle opened a bookshop and publishing house in 1791. His authors included Samuel Taylor Coleridge and the local poet Robert Southey, who was born in Wine Street in 1774.

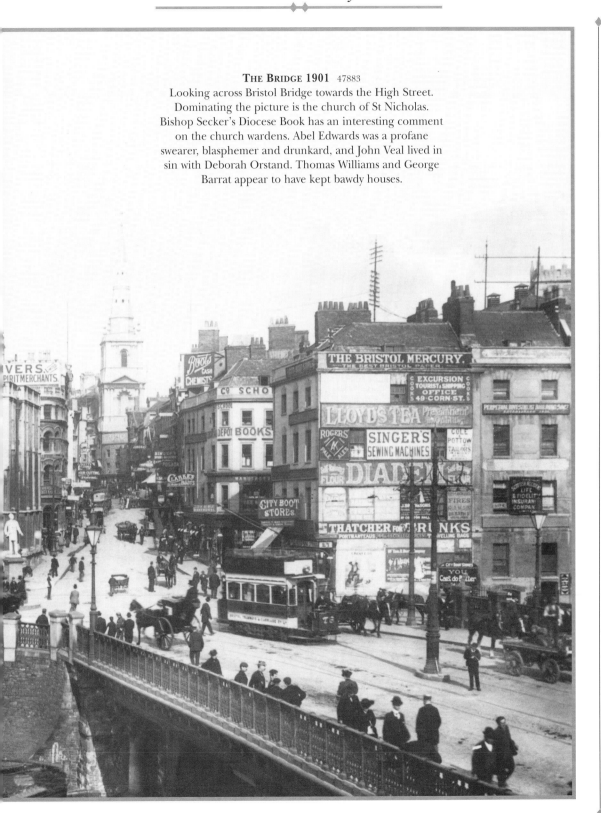

THE BRIDGE 1901 47883
Looking across Bristol Bridge towards the High Street.
Dominating the picture is the church of St Nicholas.
Bishop Secker's Diocese Book has an interesting comment
on the church wardens. Abel Edwards was a profane
swearer, blasphemer and drunkard, and John Veal lived in
sin with Deborah Orstand. Thomas Williams and George
Barrat appear to have kept bawdy houses.

THE VICTORIA ROOMS c1950 B212253
Designed by Charles Dyer, the Victoria Rooms were built between 1838 and 1842. It was here, in June 1874, that a meeting was held to thrash out proposals whereby a university college might be established in the city. The college opened in 1876 in two houses in Park Row with just 87 day students and 234 evening students.

CHRISTMAS STEPS c1950 B212193
Christmas Steps are just behind Quay Street, and are thought to have been built in the 1660s. When this picture was taken, the Steps had long enjoyed a reputation as the place to go for antiques or to seek out old books.

CHRISTMAS STEPS c1950 B212263
It was at the top of the Steps that John Foster founded an almshouse and chapel in 1481. The chapel, which was
heavily restored in the 1880s, has an unusual dedication to the Three Kings of Cologne.

CHRISTMAS STREET c1950 B212294

By the 1530s the old hospital of St Bartholomew had seen better days, and the decision was taken to convert it into a grammar school. The buildings and lands were eventually made over to the Corporation who were to act as governors. But Corporations being what they are, the lands were sold off and the school suffered accordingly.

BROADMEAD c1950 B212286

Here we see a mixture of Georgian, Victorian, thirties' style cinema, and postwar reconstruction.

BROADMEAD C1960 B212322

Broadmead runs between St James' and the Old Market Place, and was a part of the regeneration of the city centre following the destruction of the Second World War. Redevelopment entailed the demolition of some of Bristol's older buildings, including the Ebenezer Chapel of 1795, and the extension of Broadmead to incorporate Rosemary Street.

YE LLANDOGER TROW C1950 B212275

King Street still retains many 17th and 18th century buildings, despite attempts by the Luftwaffe to destroy them. Here we see the Llandoger Trow Inn, whilst a little way down the street is the Theatre Royal, home of the Bristol Old Vic since 1946.

GEORGES & CO'S
OLD BEERS
ALES AND STOUT.

THE OLD THEATRE 1890 24640
The Theatre Royal opened in 1766 and was modelled on
Christopher Wren's Drury Lane Theatre in London. Also to
be found in King Street in 1890 were the St Nicholas
Almshouse, founded in 1656, complete with its own chapel,
and the Merchant Adventurer's Almshouses, built in 1699.
The latter was restored following damage sustained during
the Blitz; St Nicholas' was extensively restored in
the early 1960s.

MERCHANT STREET c1960 B212324
Merchant Street following its redevelopment. The street was extended northwards so as to absorb Old King Street.

UNION STREET c1960 B212326
It was to this street, in 1793, that Joseph Storrs Fry moved his chocolate-making business. The business was founded by Joseph's father, who had come to Bristol from Wiltshire. Joseph Fry Senior had been involved in a number of business ventures and partnerships, but as a Quaker, the manufacture of chocolate was especially important to him, as it was a temperance drink.

ST PETER'S HOSPITAL 1901 46499

In 1712 St Peter's Hospital looked after around three hundred sick and poor people. It was under the management of the Bristol Corporation for the Poor. Times were hard and the Corporation petitioned Parliament for permission to increase the rates. To support their cause they even commissioned a census.

ROYAL VICTORIA CONVALESCENT HOME 1901 46498

One of Bristol's more flamboyant characters was Richard Smith, chief surgeon at the Royal Infirmary, and a councillor from 1835 to 1843. His hobby was to write a rhyme relating to the career of every local criminal who had been executed and then sent to him for dissection. He would then bind the pages in the skin of the unfortunate felon.

MULLER'S ORPHAN HOUSES 1901 46496

George Muller's Orphanage on Ashley Down. Prussian-born Muller arrived in Bristol in 1833 and started his orphanage three years later. As well as being a philanthropist, George was also a pastor with the Plymouth Brethren and undertook preaching tours throughout the world. He died in 1892 at the ripe old age of ninety-two.

TEMPLE CHURCH 1887 20129

In 1115, Hugue de Payens and Godfrey de Saint Adhemar founded a small group of Christian knights dedicated to the protection of pilgrims making the journey between Jericho and Jerusalem. The group was known as the Poor Knights of Christ, but it would later become the powerful Knights Templar. A small preceptory was established at Bristol during the late 12th century, and when the Order was suppressed in the 14th century the Temple Church, seen here in 1887, became the Holy Cross parish church.

GENERAL VIEW 1900 45563
A view over the rooftops of Bristol. To the right of the cathedral
can be seen something of the warehouses and wharves of the city
docks. In the centre of the picture, to the left of the church spire,
is one of the cone-shaped furnaces of a glassworks, somewhat akin
to the bottlekilns of the Potteries. In 1793 Bristol had at least a
dozen glassworks, producing a wide variety of glass and bottles for
customers throughout the West Country.

THE CEMETERY 1887 20139
Opened in 1836 by the Bristol General Cemetery Co, Arno Vale became the city's main burial ground until
augmented by the opening of Greenbank Cemetery during the 1870s. Arno Vale was laid out in terraces, and
Charles Underwood designed its Doric lodges and classical chapels.

VIEW FROM BRANDON HILL 1896 38168

At various times between 1795 and 1840 the Corporation banned the use of the Guildhall for any type of meeting they considered to be Radical. As Bristolians had enjoyed free access rights to Brandon Hill since the 16th century, the Radicals simply held their meetings there, attracting large crowds; they were almost impossible to police.

THE PARK c1950 B212293

Leisure time within the city, though it is unlikely that the Frith cameraman would have hung around long enough to see if the fish were biting. This is one of a series of photographs taken by Frith for possible use as a postcard.

THE PARK c1950 B212288

From the same sequence as the previous photo, and once again taken with a view to being published as a postcard.

THE PARK c1950 B212291

A small boy rattles along the pathway on his tricycle while older members of the community seek shelter from the sun. Once again this picture was taken for possible publication in the Frith postcard range.

ENTRANCE TO THE DOCKS c1950 B212186
The entrance lock to the Floating Harbour. In 1801-02 engineer William Jessop came up with his own designs for a tide-free city dock area that would enclose the Avon from Rownham to St Philip's. The river itself would be diverted by means of a New Cut from Totterdown to the entrance of the Floating Harbour. The project was completed by 1809, at a cost of about £600,000, with French prisoners of war being used for much of the manual labour.

ENTRANCE TO THE DOCKS 1900 45555
Even at this late date there were people advocating the 'dockisation'
of the Avon, which would have resulted in the destruction of much
of the natural beauty of the Gorge and the wholesale removal of
Horseshoe Bend so that larger vessels could come up to the city. We
may be thankful that it was decided that the facilities at Avonmouth
should be extended instead.

CLIFTON, THE SUSPENSION BRIDGE 1887 20167

A paddle tug prepares to get under way again after bringing a vessel up the Avon. The tugs greatly improved the ship-handling capabilities of the City Docks, and were far more efficient than the old rowed towboats.

THE CENTRE c1950 B212266

A view from the Centre towards St Augustine's Reach. The Reach dates from the 13th century and used to extend further into the town. When it was built in 1248 it was an outstanding piece of civil engineering for its time, as it involved the diverting of the River Frome from its junction with the Avon at Bristol Bridge. The Reach established Bristol as the major port on the west coast.

THE HARBOUR c1950 B212181

THE HARBOUR c1950

The City Docks. In the days of sail, vessels making their way up the Avon to Bristol had to contend with several problems: the current, the wind through the Gorge, and the serpentine course of the river itself. Vessels were assisted by towboats usually manned by ten or more rowers, and depending on the size of the ship and the prevailing conditions, anything up to ten towboats might be needed. In the 1770s the cost of bringing even a small vessel up the river from Pill could cost in the region of £10.

◆

THE DOCKS c1950

In 1823 the Chamber of Commerce were so concerned about the high cost of the port dues being demanded by the Bristol Dock Co that they inquired as to what charges would be levied at other ports for the same cargoes. At Bristol the dues would be £515,608, at Liverpool £231,800, at London £210,098 and at Hull £147,587. No wonder the port was losing trade.

THE DOCKS c1950 B212220

VIEW FROM THE GRANARY 1901 47880
In 1897 the Dominion Line began a weekly scheduled service
between Bristol and Canada, with the result that the importation
of grain through the docks expanded. In that year the 'Montcalm'
arrived at Avonmouth carrying over 6,000 tons of grain, which was
the largest bulk cargo the docks had then handled.

THE DOCKS 1953 B212278

During the early decades of the 19th century, Bristol was losing trade to Hull, Liverpool, London and the South Wales ports owing to high dock charges. In 1833 the cost to discharge sugar and tobacco at Bristol was double that of Liverpool. By the mid 1840s it was cheaper to discharge goods at Liverpool, and then transport them by rail to Bristol, than it was to discharge them at the Bristol docks.

THE DOCKS 1953 B212281

In the 1870s a railway line was built to serve the city docks. Though it was less than one mile long, it was expensive to build, requiring three bridges, a viaduct and a 282 yard-long tunnel under a burial ground, the cutting of which entailed the digging up of numerous former residents of Bristol and reburying them in a new cemetery at Brislington.

THE NEW BASCULE BRIDGE c1950 B212243

Today the speed limit within the Floating Harbour is 6mph, and craft proceeding under the Prince Street, Redcliffe or Bristol Bridges should sound one prolonged blast on their horn before doing so.

THE QUAY 1887 20133
This photograph was taken three years after Avonmouth,
Portishead and the city docks were brought under Corporation
control. Bristol's two principal shipping companies were the
Bristol Steam Navigation, founded in 1836 to take advantage of
the Irish trade, and the Bristol City Lines, who were both owners
and builders, with routes to South America and the East.

AVONMOUTH DOCKS 1901 46494

The earliest scheme for a non-tidal basin at Avonmouth capable of taking vessels too large to reach Bristol was a £1.5 million project promoted in 1852. Alas, it got nowhere, but work did begin in 1868 on a single basin. After running into financial difficulties on several occasions, it eventually opened in 1877. While this was going on a rival scheme was being promoted at Portishead.

AVONMOUTH DOCKS 1901 46493

In 1900 it was decided that the cargo handling and berthing facilities at Avonmouth needed upgrading so that the larger steamers then being built could use the port. Work began in 1902 on a new basin, and it was opened by King Edward VII in July 1908. The Royal Edward dock had a water area of 25 acres and a graving dock 875ft in length.

CLIFTON, THE SUSPENSION BRIDGE c1950 C120189
In 1752, William Vick bequeathed money towards the eventual bridging of the Gorge. It was not until 1829 that a competition was held for engineers and architects to submit designs. Despite entries from the likes of Thomas Telford, the competition was won by the still relatively inexperienced Isambard Kingdom Brunel.

CLIFTON
The Suspension Bridge 1887 20164
By 1843 work on the bridge had
ground to a halt, and the kitty was
empty; all the available money had
been used up on building the
abutments. It was not until 1864
that the bridge was finally
completed. The chains used to
support the road were bought
second hand, having been used on
the old Hungerford Bridge
in London.

CLIFTON, THE SUSPENSION BRIDGE 1887 20168
The bridge has a total length of 1,352ft, while the distance between the piers is 702ft. It is 31ft wide and the roadway is 245ft above the high water level, so there is little chance of a ship colliding with it.

CLIFTON, LEIGH WOODS 1887 20175
The view from the suspension bridge towards Leigh Woods. The railway line on the left is the single track Bristol & Portishead Pier & Railway which was acquired by the Great Western Railway in 1884, having been converted to standard gauge in January 1880.

VIEW FROM CLIFTON BRIDGE C1960 B212312
The view from the suspension bridge looking toward the entrance lock to the Floating Harbour, and the junction lock of the New Cut and the Cumberland Basin.

CLIFTON, THE SUSPENSION BRIDGE 1897 38157
Bristol is where Brunel's steamships 'Great Western' and 'Great Britain' were built, though both were too big to use the Floating Harbour. Both ships drew large crowds when they were first towed out of Bristol and through the Gorge.

CLIFTON, GRANBY HILL AND ST VINCENT'S PARK 1887 20162

As Clifton's reputation as a resort grew, the late Georgian terraces were built in a style that deliberately imitated Bath. Using Bath stone for the facings, the whole scheme was topped off with a series of splendid crescents offering superb views of the Gorge and surrounding countryside.

CLIFTON, THE COLLEGE 1887 20179
Clifton College became the most famous of all Bristol's schools. Founded in 1860 and opened in 1862, Charles Hanson designed the original buildings, including the Great Hall. The school's first headmaster, John Percival, is acknowledged as being responsible for making Clifton one of the leading schools of the day.

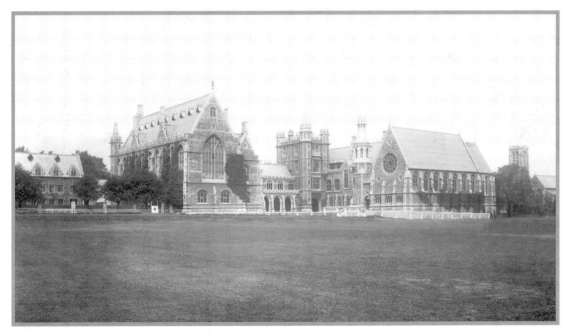

CLIFTON, THE COLLEGE 1901 46503
The college admitted both boarders and town boys, and somewhat uniquely for the period, regarded them all with equal status. Clifton was one of the first schools to teach engineering, and under headmaster James Wilson (1879-1890) the teaching of science was greatly improved.

CLIFTON
from the Downs **1896** 38165
Here we see the roofs of Clifton from the pleasantly wooded
Downs. The Downs became as important to the resort as were
the Hotwells; a favourite haunt for artists and visitors interested
in the geology, flora and fauna of the area.

THE ZOO C1960 B212311
Bristol Zoo has its home in Clifton and was founded in 1835.

KEYNSHAM, HIGH STREET 1950 K64003
On 26 June 1685 the village was the scene of a skirmish between 350 royalist troops and rebel forces of the Duke of Monmouth. Monmouth lost his nerve and turned away from Bristol. On arriving at Bath, Monmouth sent a messenger to the town to demand the surrender of the local garrison. The town's answer was to shoot the messenger dead.

HENBURY, BLAISE CASTLE c1955 H164303
Blaise Castle was built as a folly by Thomas Farr, Master of the Society of Merchant Venturers. In 1765 Thomas had been a member of a delegation sent by the Merchant Venturers to deliver a petition against the renewal of the Sugar Act; the government intended to use it to make the American colonies pay for their own defence. The merchants' close links with the Americans made them realize the Act would harm relations and damage trade. They were right.

HENBURY, THE POST OFFICE c1955 H164001

The Blaise Inn receives a pre-summer season coat of paint. The George Brewery was established in 1702, and was owned and run by the George family from 1788 until 1961 when it was bought by Courage. Now a part of Scottish Courage, Georges' Bitter Ale is still on sale, though it is unusual to find it outside the West Country or Southeast Wales.

HENBURY c1955 H164006

Nearby is Blaise Castle House which even in the 1920s had the best golf course in the area; green fees were 3s, Sunday play was available, and members of the ladies golf union were permitted. On the right of the picture is the village post office and shop.

SHIREHAMPTON, THE GEORGE INN c1955 S270004
Shirehampton is situated between Bristol and Avonmouth. In 1865 the Bristol Port & Pier Railway opened its single line between Avonmouth and Hotwells with intermediate stations at Sea Mills and Shirehampton. As this was a purely local railway, no provision had been made to connect it with any other railway. Even the opening date was kept a secret until a few minutes before the departure of the first train, for fear that the train would be overloaded; the railway only had one engine.

SHIREHAMPTON, HIGH STREET C1955 S270001
Shirehampton was eventually linked by rail to Bristol with the opening of the Clifton Extension Railway in the 1870s. With the opening of Avonmouth Docks the line soon became very busy and had to be doubled in order to cope with the traffic.

ALMONDSBURY, THE BOWL INN c1955 A103005

The Bowl Inn, when Georges' Beers was still a family run brewery. Scottish Courage's Bristol brewery is said to be the largest in the UK now dedicated to the brewing of real ale.

ALMONDSBURY, THE VILLAGE c1955 A103001

As can be seen here, roads in the mid-1950s were a lot quieter than they are today. In 1955 UK car production reached a new record of nearly 900,000 cars and home sales were counted at over 500,000. Suddenly in November the Chancellor increased the purchase tax on new cars by 50 to 60 per cent in order to suppress the growing demand.

PORTISHEAD
The Esplanade **1924** 76002
The Bristol & Portishead Pier & Railway was a single broad-
gauge line, which opened in April 1867, and connected with
the Bristol & Exeter Railway at Bedminster. The pier opened
in June 1868 and was soon extended so vessels could use it at
low water. From Portishead there was a year-round steamer
service to Cardiff and Newport and summer sailings
to Ilfracombe.

Index

Almondsbury 85

Avonmouth Docks 70

Blaise Castle 81

Bristol Bridge 42-43

Bristol Cathedral 23, 24-25, 26, 27

Bristol Park 57, 58

Bristol Theatre 48-49

Broad Street 40

Broadmead 46, 47

Cabot Tower 22

Cemetery 56

Christmas Steps 44, 45, 46

City Centre 33, 38, 39, 40, 62

Clifton 78-79

Clifton College 77

Clifton Suspension Bridge 60-61, 62, 71, 72-73, 74, 75, 76

College Green 28

Docks 59, 63, 64-65, 66, 67

Granby Hill 76

Henbury 82

Keynsham 80

Leigh Woods 74

Merchant Street 50

Muller's Orphan Houses 52

Park Street 29, 30-31

Portishead 86-87

Quay 68-69

Queen's Road 32

Royal Victoria Convalescent Home 52

Shirehampton 83, 84

St Augustine's Bridge 33, 34-35, 36-37

St Mary Redcliffe Church 18-19, 20, 21

St Peter's Hospital 51

Temple Church 53

Tolley's Bank 41

Union Street 50

University 32

Victoria Rooms 44

Ye Llandoger Trow 47

Zoo 80

Frith Book Co 1999 Titles

From 2000 we aim at publishing 100 new books each year. For latest catalogue please contact Frith Book Co

Barnstaple	1-85937-084-5	£12.99	Oct 99
Blackpool	1-85937-049-7	£12.99	Sep 99
Bognor Regis	1-85937-055-1	£12.99	Sep 99
Bristol	1-85937-050-0	£12.99	Sep 99
Cambridge	1-85937-092-6	£12.99	Oct 99
Cambridgeshire	1-85937-086-1	£14.99	Nov 99
Cheshire	1-85937-045-4	£14.99	Sep 99
Chester	1-85937-090-X	£12.99	Nov 99
Chesterfield	1-85937-071-3	£12.99	Sep 99
Chichester	1-85937-089-6	£12.99	Nov 99
Cornwall	1-85937-054-3	£14.99	Sep 99
Cotswolds	1-85937-099-3	£14.99	Nov 99

Maidstone	1-85937-056-X	£12.99	Sep 99
Northumberland & Tyne and Wear	1-85937-072-1	£14.99	Sep 99
North Yorkshire	1-85937-048-9	£14.99	Sep 99
Nottingham	1-85937-060-8	£12.99	Sep 99
Oxfordshire	1-85937-076-4	£14.99	Oct 99
Penzance	1-85937-069-1	£12.99	Sep 99
Reading	1-85937-087-X	£12.99	Nov 99
St Ives	1-85937-068-3	£12.99	Sep 99
Salisbury	1-85937-091-8	£12.99	Nov 99
Scarborough	1-85937-104-3	£12.99	Sep 99
Scottish Castles	1-85937-077-2	£14.99	Oct 99
Sevenoaks and Tonbridge	1-85937-057-8	£12.99	Sep 99
Sheffield and S Yorkshire	1-85937-070-5	£12.99	Sep 99
Shropshire	1-85937-083-7	£14.99	Nov 99
Southampton	1-85937-088-8	£12.99	Nov 99
Staffordshire	1-85937-047-0	£14.99	Sep 99
Stratford upon Avon	1-85937-098-5	£12.99	Nov 99
Suffolk	1-85937-074-8	£14.99	Oct 99
Surrey	1-85937-081-0	£14.99	Oct 99
Torbay	1-85937-063-2	£12.99	Sep 99
Wiltshire	1-85937-053-5	£14.99	Sep 99

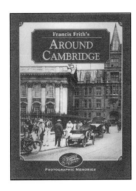

Derby	1-85937-046-2	£12.99	Sep 99
Devon	1-85937-052-7	£14.99	Sep 99
Dorset	1-85937-075-6	£14.99	Oct 99
Dorset Coast	1-85937-062-4	£14.99	Sep 99
Dublin	1-85937-058-6	£12.99	Sep 99
East Anglia	1-85937-059-4	£14.99	Sep 99
Eastbourne	1-85937-061-6	£12.99	Sep 99
English Castles	1-85937-078-0	£14.99	Oct 99
Essex	1-85937-082-9	£14.99	Nov 99
Falmouth	1-85937-066-7	£12.99	Sep 99
Hampshire	1-85937-064-0	£14.99	Sep 99
Hertfordshire	1-85937-079-9	£14.99	Nov 99
Isle of Man	1-85937-065-9	£14.99	Sep 99
Liverpool	1-85937-051-9	£12.99	Sep 99

British Life A Century Ago

246 x 189mm
144pp, hardback.
Black and white
Lavishly illustrated with photos from the turn of the century, and with extensive commentary. It offers a unique insight into the social history and heritage of bygone Britain.

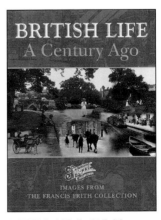

1-85937-103-5 £17.99 ....

Available from your local bookshop or from the publisher

FRITH PRODUCTS & SERVICES

Francis Frith would doubtless be pleased to know that the pioneering publishing venture he started in 1860 still continues today. More than a hundred and thirty years later, The Francis Frith Collection continues in the same innovative tradition and is now one of the foremost publishers of vintage photographs in the world. Some of the current activities include:

Interior Decoration

Today Frith's photographs can be seen framed and as giant wall murals in thousands of pubs, restaurants, hotels, banks, retail stores and other public buildings throughout the country. In every case they enhance the unique local atmosphere of the places they depict and provide reminders of gentler days in an increasingly busy and frenetic world.

Product Promotions

Frith products have been used by many major companies to promote the sales of their own products or to reinforce their own history and heritage. Brands include Hovis bread, Courage beers, Scots Porage Oats, Colman's mustard, Cadbury's foods, Mellow Birds coffee, Dunhill pipe tobacco, Guinness, and Bulmer's Cider.

Genealogy and Family History

As the interest in family history and roots grows world-wide, more and more people are turning to Frith's photographs of Great Britain for images of the towns, villages and streets where their ancestors lived; and, of course, photographs of the churches and chapels where their ancestors were christened, married and buried are an essential part of every genealogy tree and family album.

A series of easy-to-use CD Roms is planned for publication, and an increasing number of Frith photographs will be able to be viewed on specialist genealogy sites. A growing range of Frith books will be available on CD.

The Internet

Already thousands of Frith photographs can be viewed and purchased on the internet. By the end of the year 2000 some 60,000 Frith photographs will be available on the internet. The number of sites is constantly expanding, each focussing on different products and services from the Collection.

Some of the sites are listed below.

www.townpages.co.uk
www.familystorehouse.com
www.britannia.com
www.icollector.com
www.barclaysquare.co.uk
www.cornwall-online.co.uk

For background information on the Collection look at the two following sites:

www.francisfrith.com
www.francisfrith.co.uk

Frith Products

All Frith photographs are available Framed or just as Mounted Prints, and can be ordered from the address below. From time to time other products - Address Books, Calendars, Table Mats, Postcards etc - are available.

The Frith Collectors' Guild

In response to the many customers who enjoy collecting Frith photographs we have created the Frith Collectors' Guild. Members are entitled to a range of benefits, including a regular magazine, special discounts and special limited edition products.

For further information: if you would like further information on any of the above aspects of the Frith business please contact us at the address below:
The Francis Frith Collection, Frith's Barn, Teffont, Salisbury, Wiltshire England SP3 5QP.
Tel: +44 (0) 1722 716 376 Fax: +44 (0) 1722 716 881 Email: frithbook.co.uk

To receive your FREE Mounted Print

Cut out this Voucher and return it with your remittance for £1.50 to cover postage and handling. Choose any photograph included in this book. Your SEPIA print will be A4 in size, and mounted in a cream mount with burgundy rule lines, overall size 14 x 11 inches.

Order additional Mounted Prints at HALF PRICE (only £7.49 each*)

If there are further pictures you would like to order, possibly as gifts for friends and family, acquire them at half price (no additional postage and handling required).

Have your Mounted Prints framed*

For an additional £14.95 per print you can have your chosen Mounted Print framed in an elegant polished wood and gilt moulding, overall size 16 x 13 inches (no additional postage and handling required).

---

* IMPORTANT!
These special prices are only available if ordered using the original voucher on this page (no copies permitted) and at the same time as your free Mounted Print, for delivery to the same address

---

Voucher for FREE and Reduced Price Frith Prints

Picture no.	Page number	Qty	Mounted @ £7.49	Framed + £14.95	Total Cost
		1	Free of charge*	£	£
			£	£	£
			£	£	£
			£	£	£
			£	£	£
			£	£	£
				* Post & handling	£1.50
Title: AROUND BRISTOL 050-0				**Total Order Cost**	£

Please do not photocopy this voucher. Only the original is valid, so please cut it out and return it to us.

I enclose a cheque / postal order for £ . . . . made payable to 'The Francis Frith Collection'
OR please debit my Mastercard / Visa / Switch / Amex card

Number . . . .

Expires . . . . Signature . . . .

Name Mr/Mrs/Ms . . . .

Address . . . .

. . . .

. . . .

. . . .

. . . . Postcode . . . .

Daytime Tel No . . . .   Valid to 31/12/01

Frith Collectors' Guild

From time to time we publish a magazine of news and stories about Frith photographs and further special offers of Frith products. If you would like 12 months FREE membership, please return this form and we will send you a New Member Pack.

Send completed forms to:
The Francis Frith Collection, Frith's Barn, Teffont, Salisbury, Wiltshire SP3 5QP

The Francis Frith Collectors' Guild

I would like to receive the New Members Pack offering 12 months FREE membership.
050-0

Name Mr/Mrs/Ms . . . .

Address . . . .

. . . .

. . . .

. . . . Postcode . . . .

Free Print - see overleaf